# Disney's

# My First Songbook

## A Treasury of Favorite Songs to Sing and Play

Disney
PRESS

New York

HAL•LEONARD®
CORPORATION

7777 W. BLUEMOUND RD. P.O. BOX 13819 MILWAUKEE, WI 53213

# Contents

# Cruella De Vil

### From Walt Disney's *101 Dalmatians*

Words and Music by Mel Leven

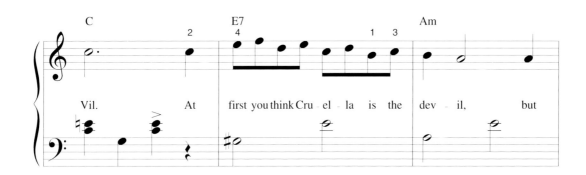

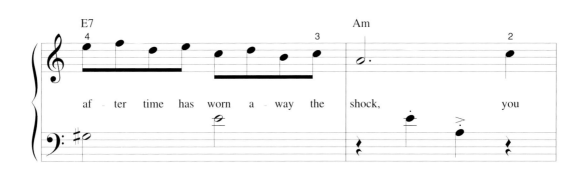

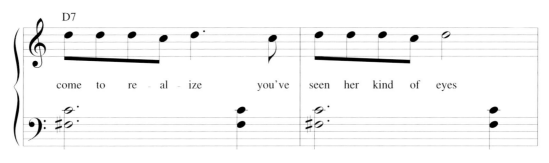

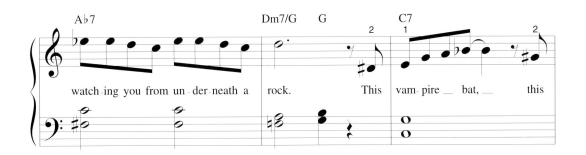

watch-ing you from un-der-neath a rock. This vam-pire — bat, — this

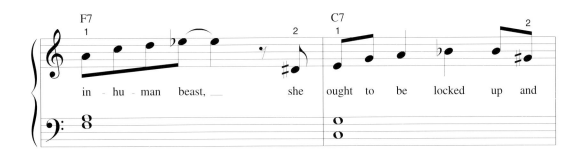

in - hu - man beast, — she ought to be locked up and

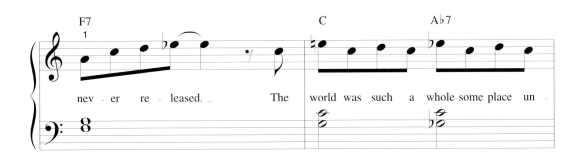

nev - er re - leased. — The world was such a whole-some place un -

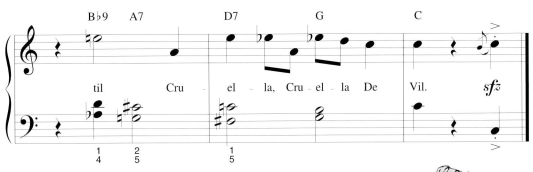

til Cru - el - la, Cru - el - la De Vil.

*sfz*

# A Whole New World

## From Walt Disney's *Aladdin*

### Music by Alan Menken • Lyrics by Tim Rice

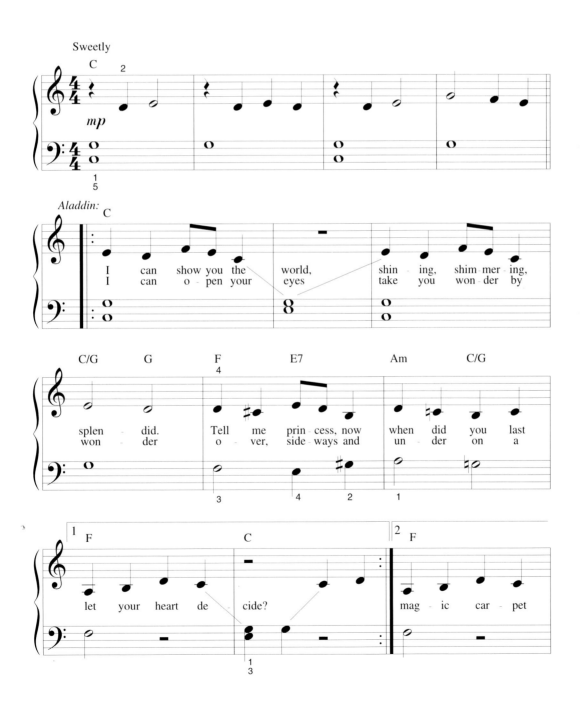

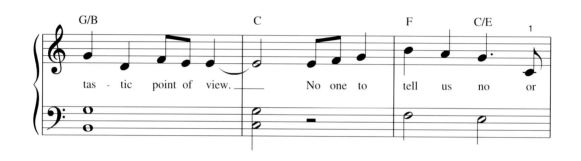

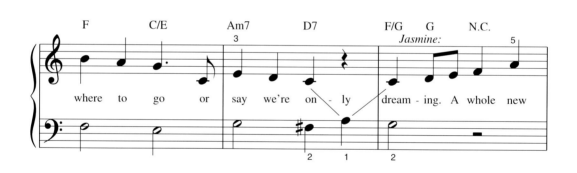

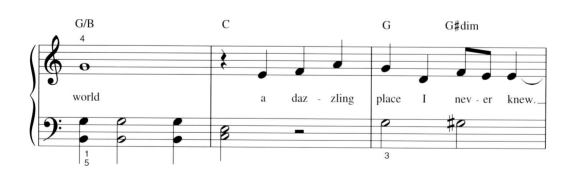

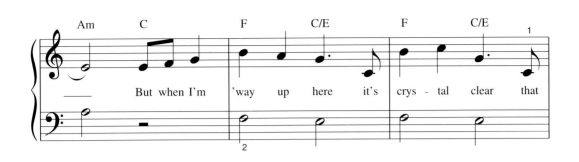

But when I'm 'way up here it's crys-tal clear that

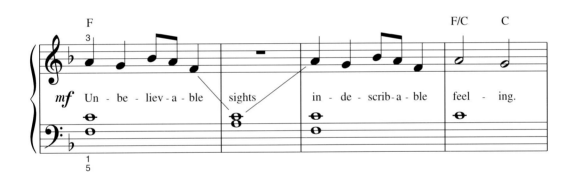

now I'm in a whole new world with you.

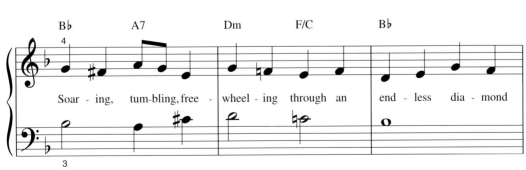

Un-be-liev-a-ble sights in-de-scrib-a-ble feel-ing.

Soar-ing, tum-bling, free-wheel-ing through an end-less dia-mond

sky.   A whole new   world, _____   a  hun - dred   thou - sand things to  see. __

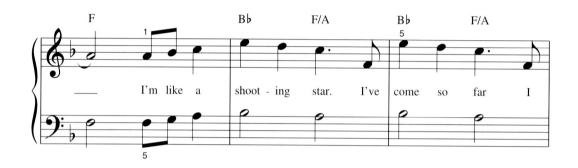

_____   I'm  like  a   shoot - ing  star.   I've  come  so  far   I

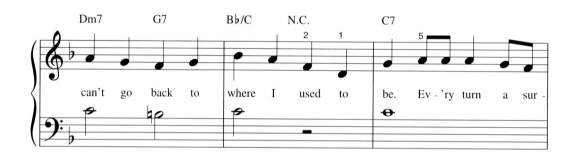

can't  go  back  to   where  I  used  to   be.  Ev - 'ry  turn  a  sur -

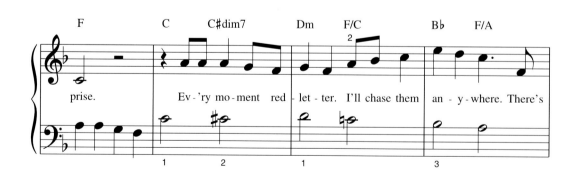

prise.   Ev - 'ry  mo - ment  red - let - ter.  I'll chase them   an - y - where. There's

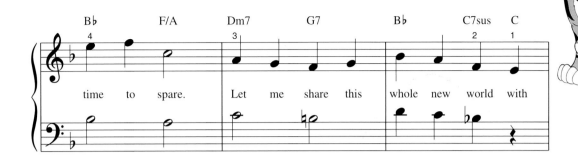

time to spare. Let me share this whole new world with

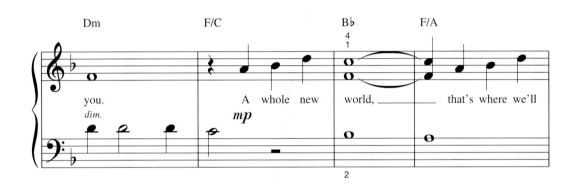

you. A whole new world, _____ that's where we'll

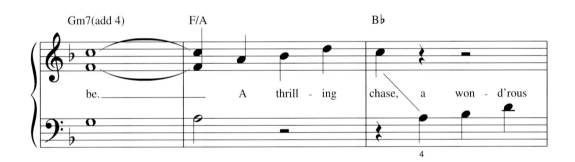

be. _____ A thrill - ing chase, a won - d'rous

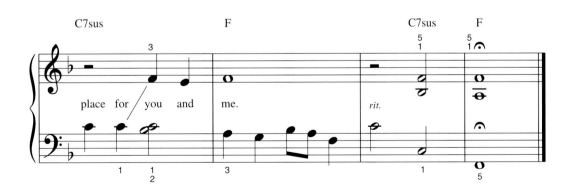

place for you and me.

# The Bare Necessities

## From Walt Disney's *The Jungle Book*

### Words and Music by Terry Gilkyson

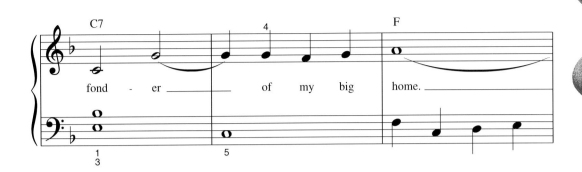

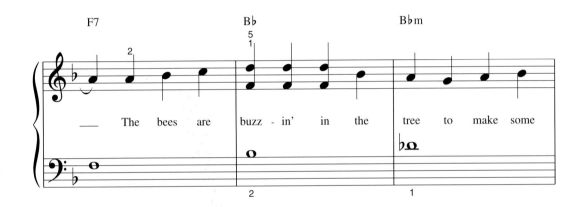

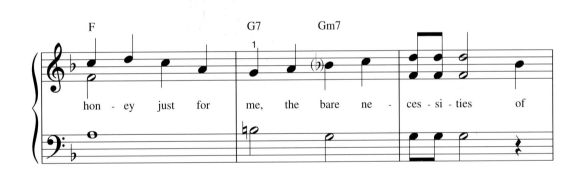

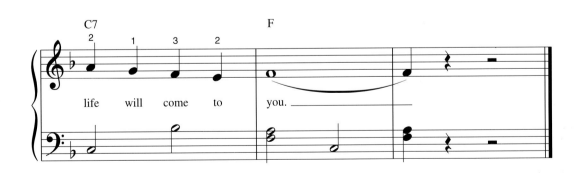

# Colors of the Wind

## From Walt Disney's *Pocahontas*

Music by Alan Menken • Lyrics by Stephen Schwartz

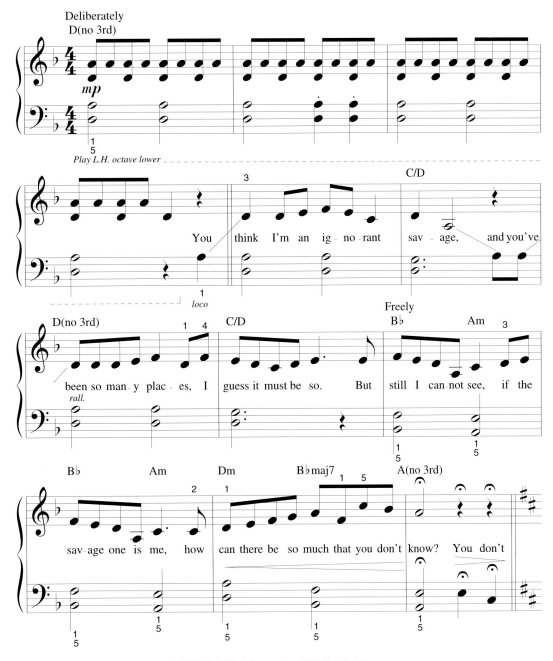

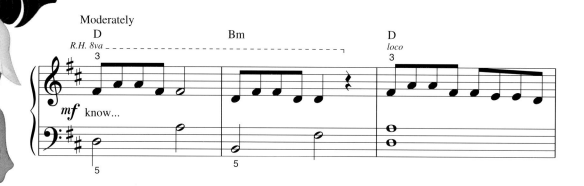

Moderately

*mf* know...

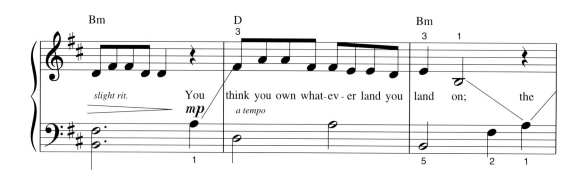

*slight rit.* You think you own what-ev-er land you land on; the

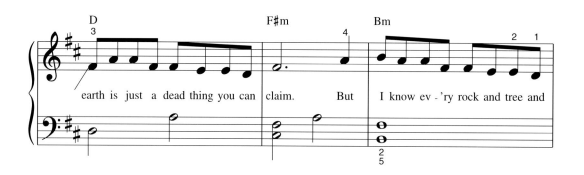

earth is just a dead thing you can claim. But I know ev-'ry rock and tree and

crea - ture has a life, has a spir - it, has a name. You

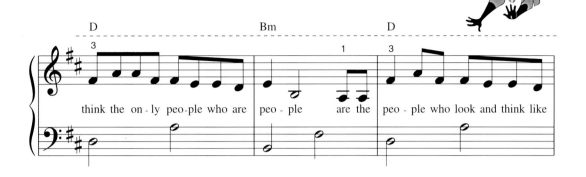

think the on - ly peo - ple who are peo - ple are the peo - ple who look and think like

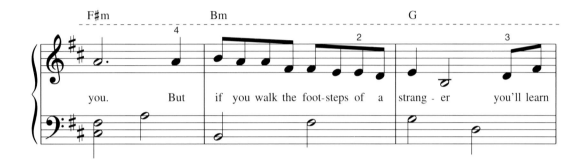

you. But if you walk the foot-steps of a strang - er you'll learn

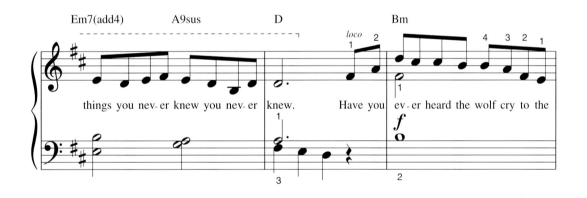

things you nev - er knew you nev - er knew. Have you ev - er heard the wolf cry to the

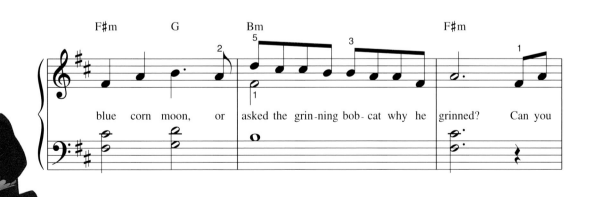

blue corn moon, or asked the grin - ning bob - cat why he grinned? Can you

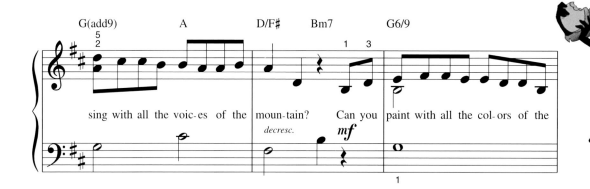

sing with all the voic-es of the | moun-tain? Can you | paint with all the col-ors of the

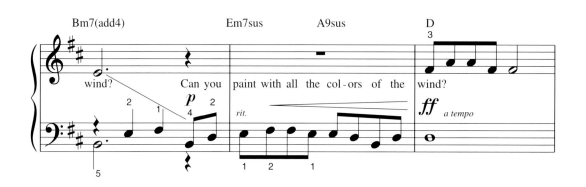

wind? | Can you | paint with all the col-ors of the | wind?

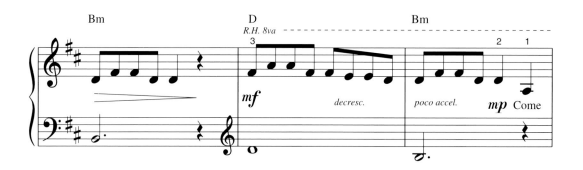

mp Come

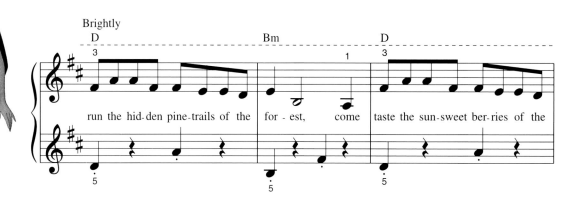

**Brightly**

run the hid-den pine-trails of the | for - est, come | taste the sun-sweet ber-ries of the

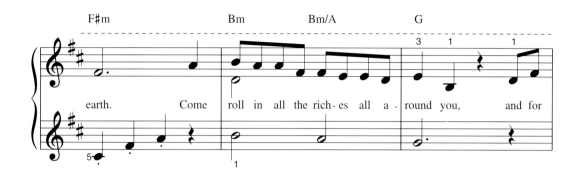

earth. Come roll in all the rich-es all a-round you, and for

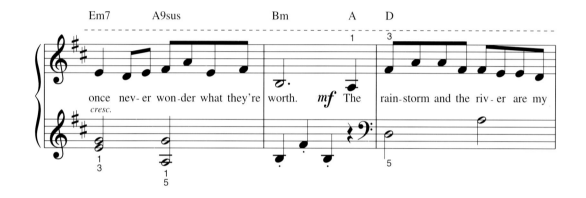

once nev-er won-der what they're worth. *mf* The rain-storm and the riv-er are my

bro-thers; the her-on and the ot-ter are my friends; and

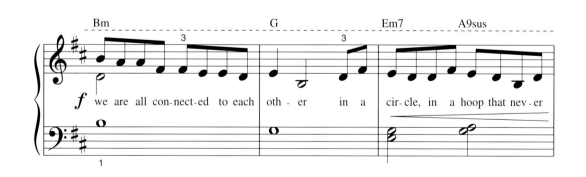

we are all con-nect-ed to each oth-er in a cir-cle, in a hoop that nev-er

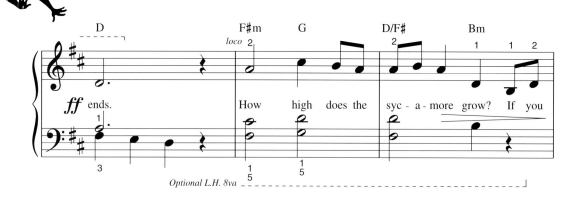

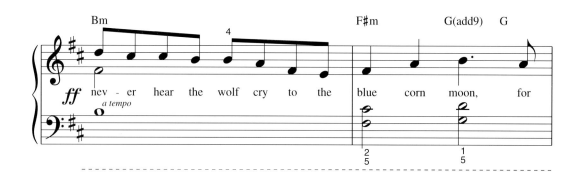

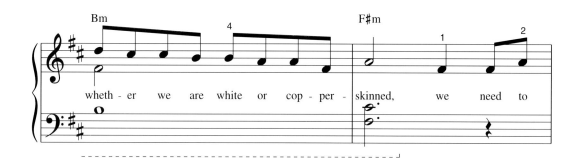

sing with all the voic-es of the moun-tain, need to paint with all the col-ors of the

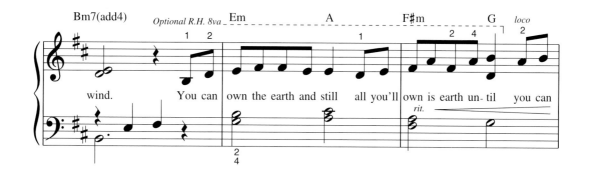

wind. You can own the earth and still all you'll own is earth un-til you can

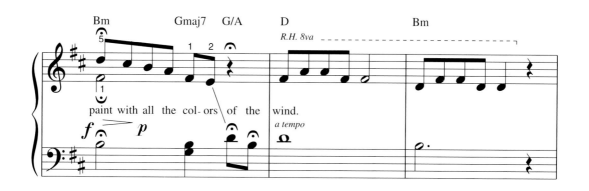

paint with all the col-ors of the wind.

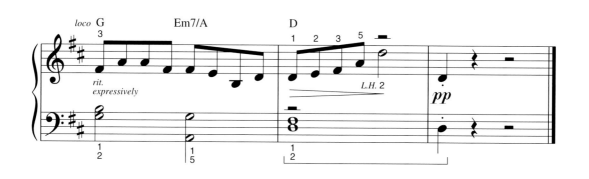

# Under the Sea

## From Walt Disney's *The Little Mermaid*

Lyrics by Howard Ashman • Music by Alan Menken

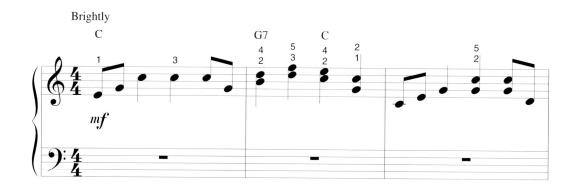

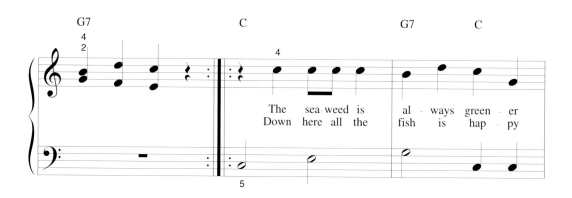

The sea-weed is
Down here all the

al - ways green - er
fish is hap - py

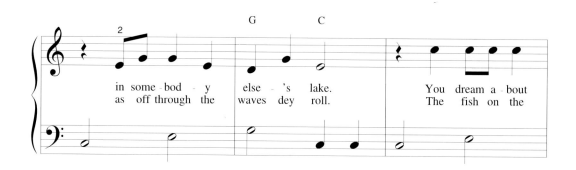

in some-bod - y
as off through the

else - 's lake.
waves dey roll.

You dream a - bout
The fish on the

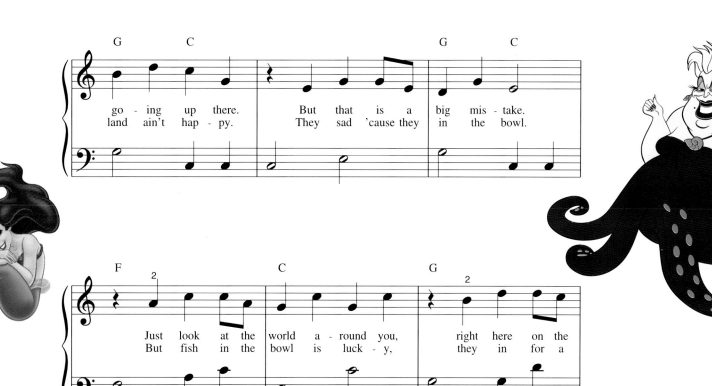

go - ing    up    there.      But   that   is   a      big   mis - take.
land  ain't hap - py.         They  sad  'cause they   in   the  bowl.

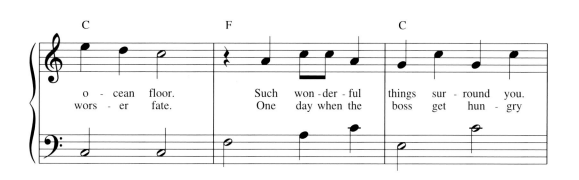

Just   look    at   the     world   a - round  you,      right  here   on  the
But   fish    in   the      bowl   is   luck - y,       they   in   for  a

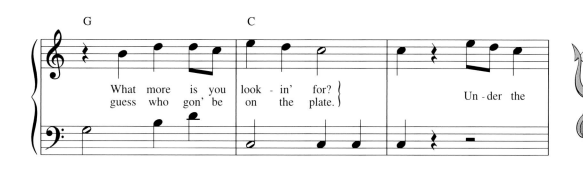

o - cean  floor.      Such   won-der-ful    things  sur - round  you.
wors - er  fate.      One    day when the   boss   get   hun - gry

What  more   is  you     look - in'   for?      Un - der the
guess  who  gon' be      on   the   plate.

28

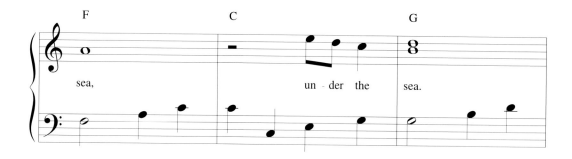

sea,         un - der the   sea.

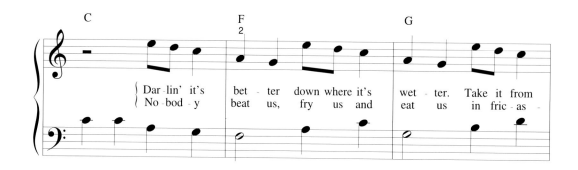

Dar -lin' it's    bet - ter   down where it's    wet - ter.   Take it from
No -bod - y    beat   us,   fry   us and     eat   us   in   fric - as -

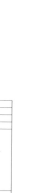

me.             Up   on   the     shore   they   work all day.
see.            We   what the     land   folks   loves to cook.

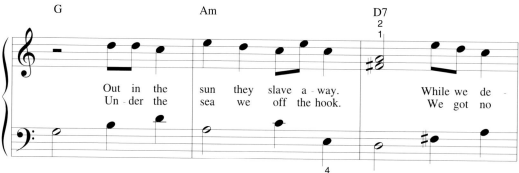

Out   in   the     sun   they   slave a - way.        While we   de -
Un - der the     sea   we     off the hook.         We got   no

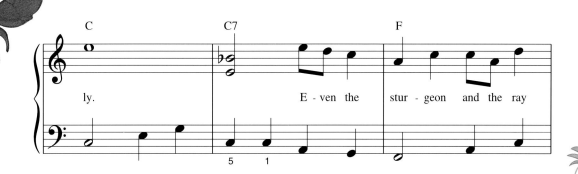

ly.                    E - ven the     stur - geon and the ray

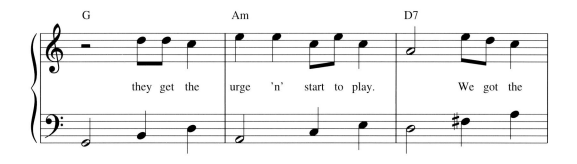

they get the    urge 'n' start to play.       We got the

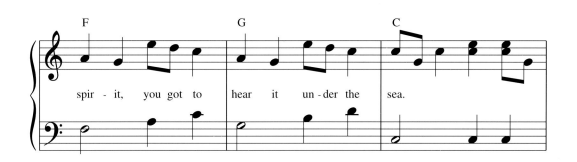

spir - it,   you got to   hear it un - der the   sea.

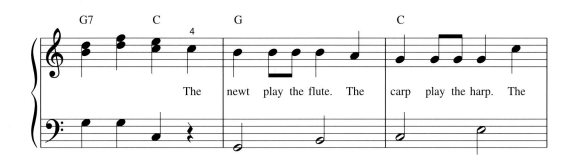

The    newt play the flute. The   carp play the harp. The

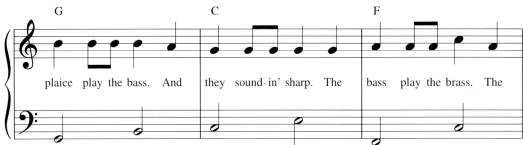

plaice play the bass. And they sound-in' sharp. The bass play the brass. The

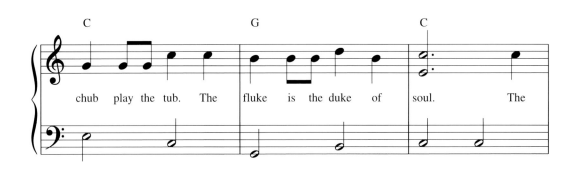

chub play the tub. The fluke is the duke of soul. The

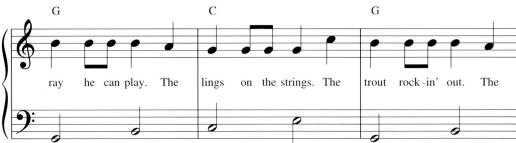

ray he can play. The lings on the strings. The trout rock-in' out. The

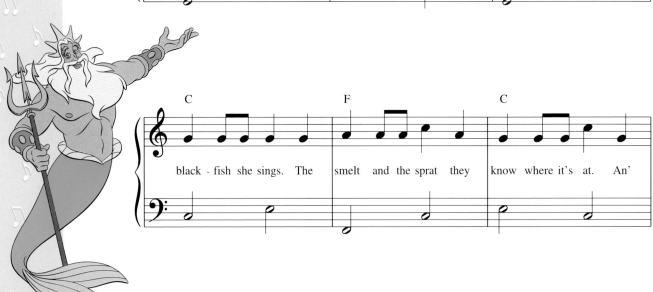

black - fish she sings. The smelt and the sprat they know where it's at. An'

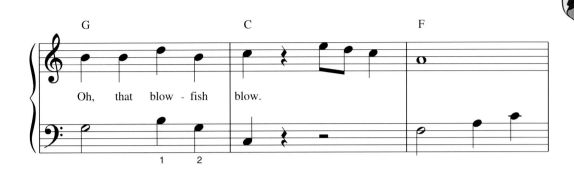

Oh,    that   blow - fish   blow.

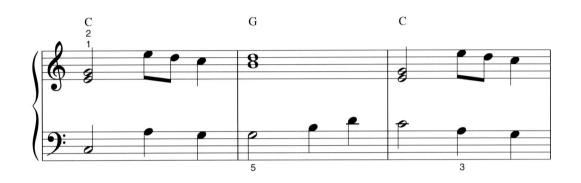

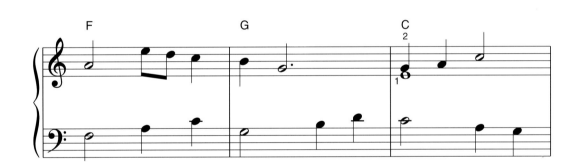

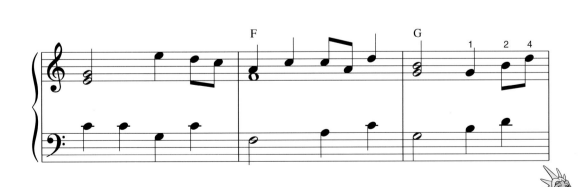

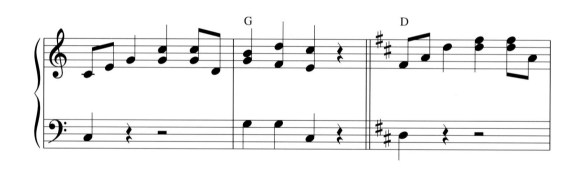

Un - der   the

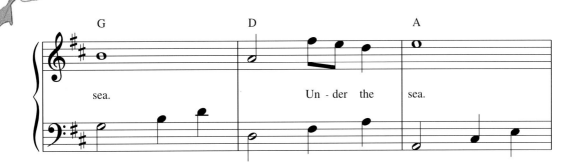

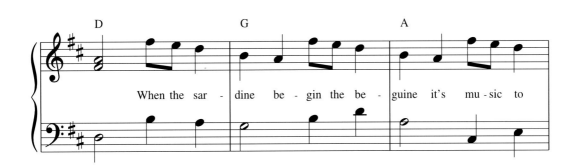

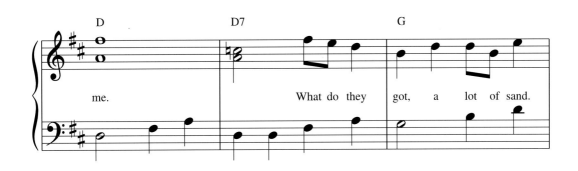

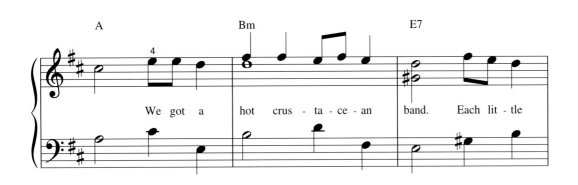

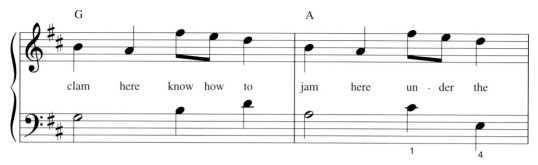

clam    here    know how    to    jam    here    un - der    the

sea.    Each    lit - tle

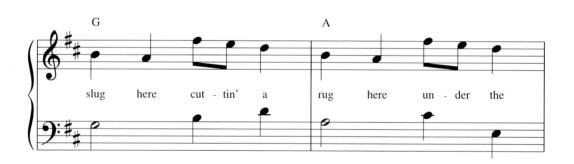

slug    here    cut - tin'    a    rug    here    un - der    the

sea.    Each    lit - tle

snail here know how to wail here. That's why it's

hot -ter un -der the wa -ter. Ya we in

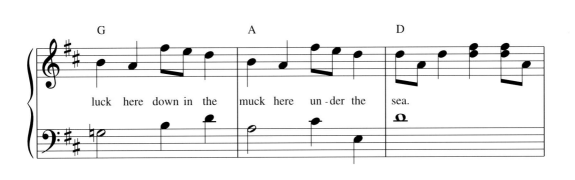

luck here down in the muck here un -der the sea.

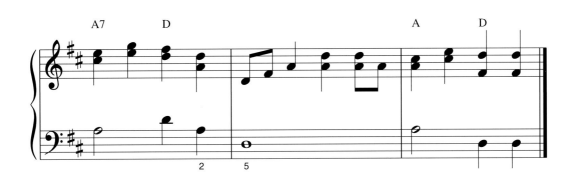

# Following the Leader

## From Walt Disney's *Peter Pan*

### Words by Ted Sears and Winston Hibler • Music by Oliver Wallace

Fol - low-ing the lead - er, the lead - er, the lead - er, we're

fol - low-ing the lead - er wher - ev - er he may go. ____ We

won't be home till morn - ing, till morn - ing, till morn - ing, we

won't be home till morn - ing be - cause he told us so. Tee

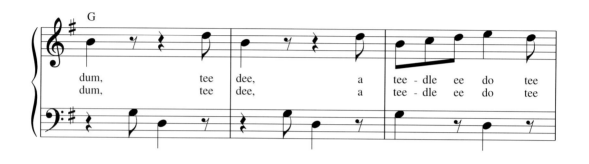

dum,      tee dee,      a tee - dle ee do tee
dum,      tee dee,      a tee - dle ee do tee

day.      We're out      for fun,      and
day.      We march for a - long, and

this is the game we play.      Come on,      join
these are the words we say:      Come Tee dum tee

in      and     sing   your   trou - bles   a -   way,      with   a
dee      a    tee - dle   dee - dle   dee -   ay,      oh,   a

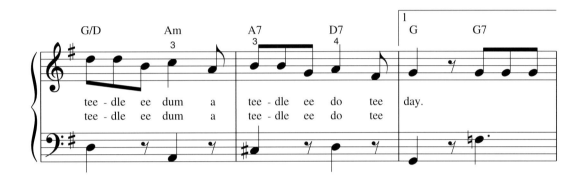

tee - dle   ee   dum   a    tee - dle   ee   do   tee    day.
tee - dle   ee   dum   a    tee - dle   ee   do   tee

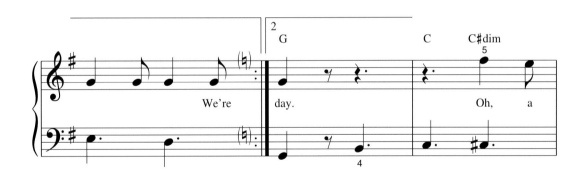

We're     day.            Oh,   a

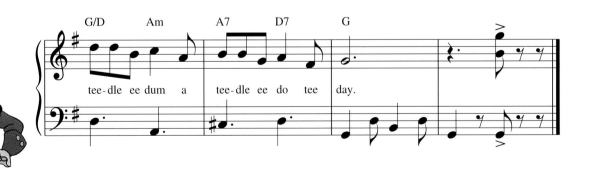

tee - dle   ee   dum   a    tee - dle   ee   do   tee    day.

41

# You've Got a Friend in Me

## From Walt Disney's *Toy Story*

### Music and Lyrics by Randy Newman

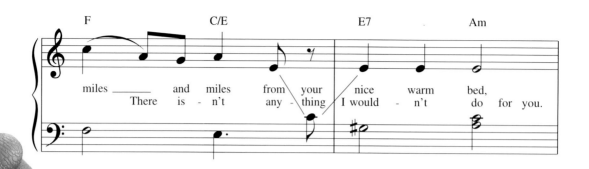

miles _____ and miles from your nice warm bed,
There is - n't any - thing I would - n't do for you.

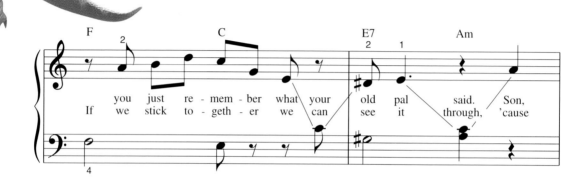

you just re - mem - ber what your old pal said. Son,
If we stick to - geth - er we can see it through, 'cause

you've got a friend in me.
you've got a friend in me. Yeah,
Yeah,

1.

you've got a friend in me.

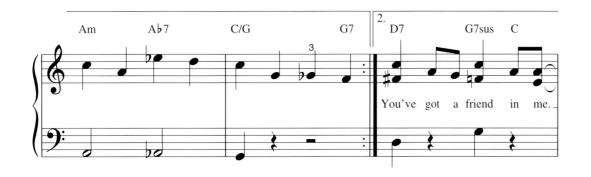

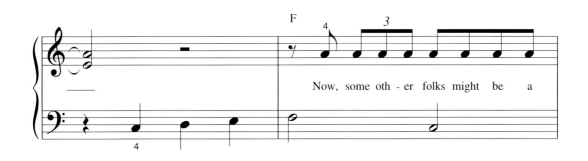

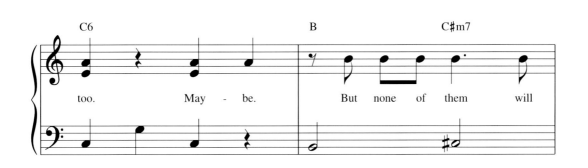

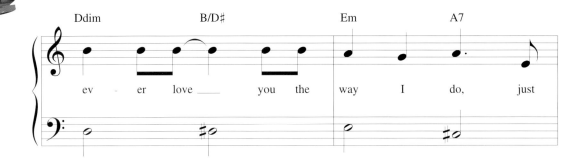

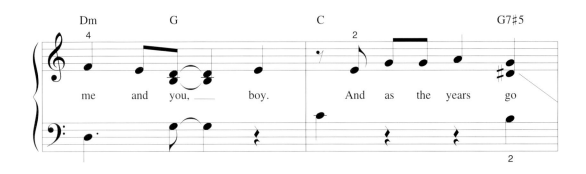

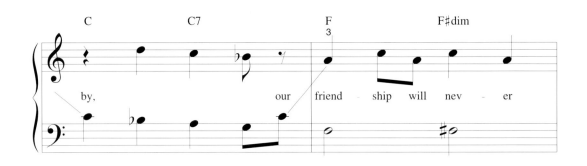

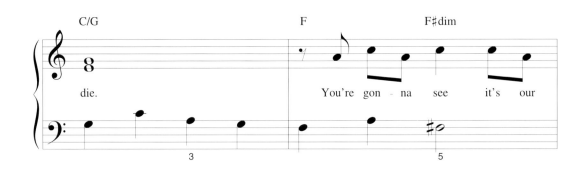

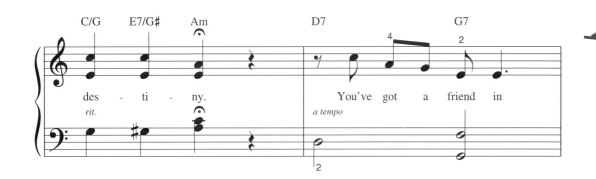

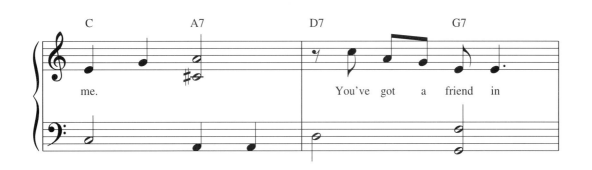

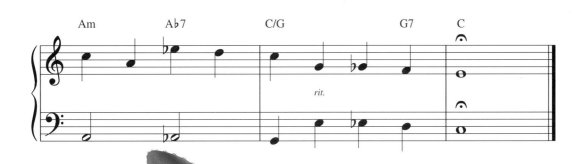

# Once Upon a Dream

## From Walt Disney's *Sleeping Beauty*

Words and Music by Sammy Fain and Jack Lawrence
Adapted from a Theme by Tchaikovsky

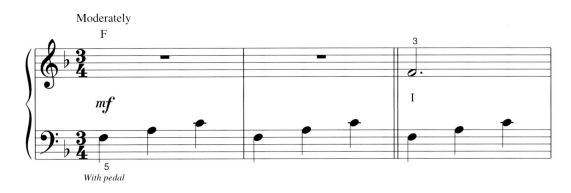

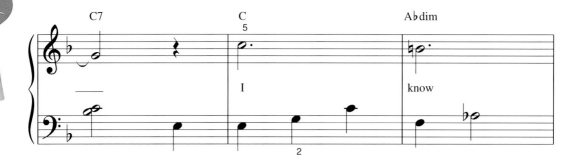

I know

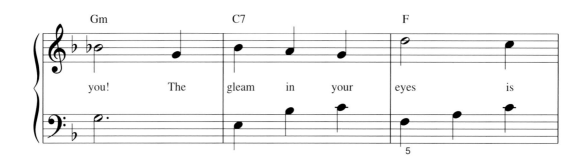

you! The gleam in your eyes is

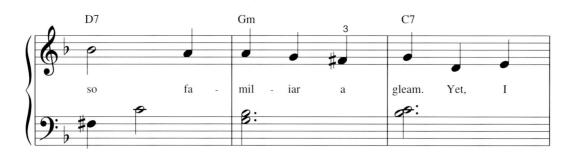

so fa - mil - iar a gleam. Yet, I

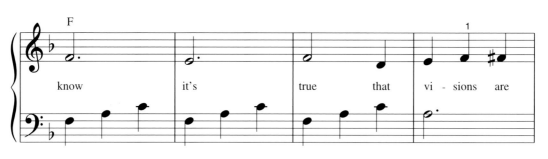

know it's true that vi - sions are

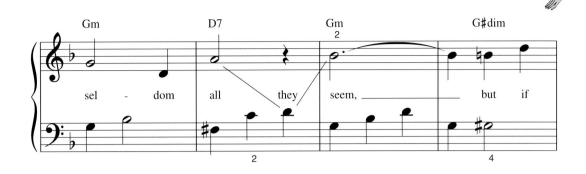

sel - dom all they seem, _____ but if

I know you, I know what you'll do: you'll

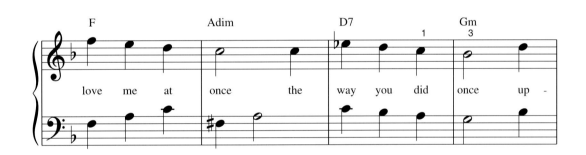

love me at once the way you did once up -

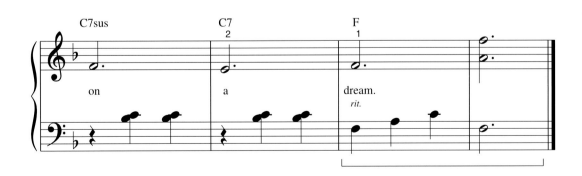

on a dream.

# A Dream Is a Wish Your Heart Makes

## From Walt Disney's *Cinderella*

Words and Music by Mack David, Al Hoffman and Jerry Livingston

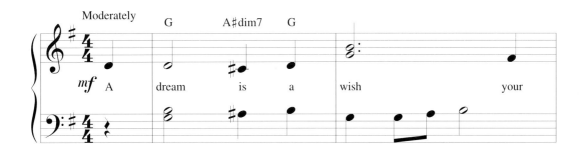

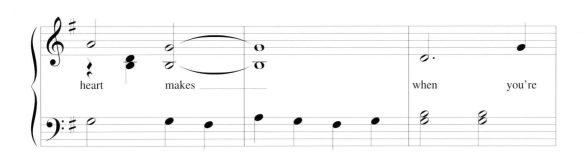

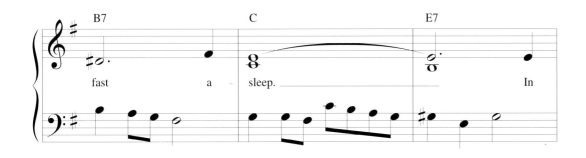

**Am** ... **Am7**

dreams    you    will    lose    your    heart    aches;

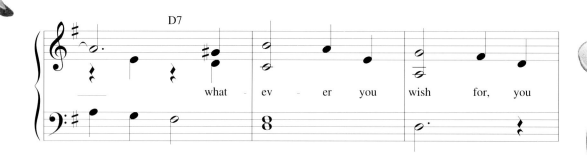

**D7**

what - ev - er  you  wish  for,  you

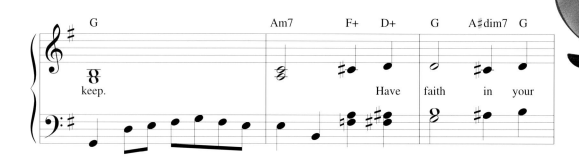

**G** ... **Am7**  **F+**  **D+**  **G**  **A#dim7**  **G**

keep.    Have  faith  in  your

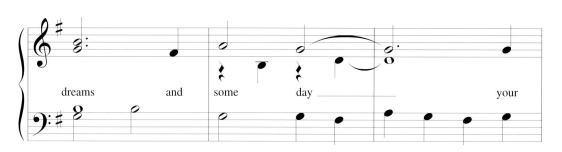

dreams    and    some    day    your

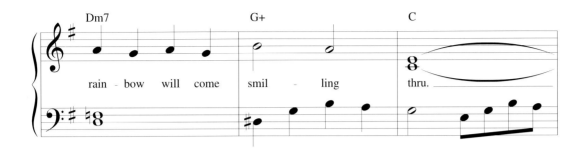

rain - bow will come smil - ling thru.

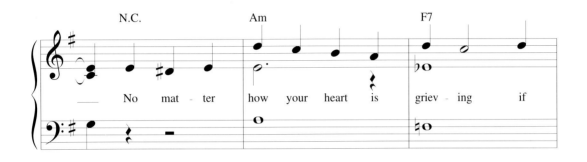

No mat - ter how your heart is griev - ing if

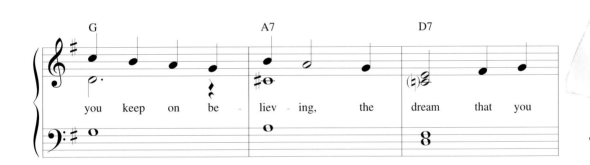

you keep on be - liev - ing, the dream that you

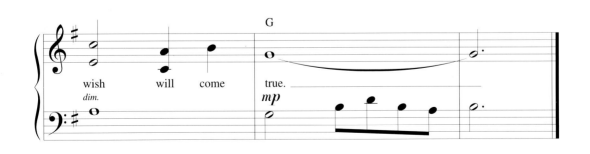

wish will come true.

*dim.*   *mp*

# Bibbidi-Bobbidi-Boo

## (The Magic Song)

### From Walt Disney's *Cinderella*

Words by Jerry Livingston • Music by Mack David and Al Hoffman

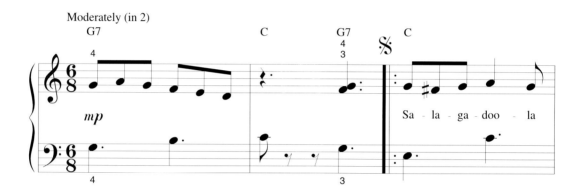

Sa - la - ga - doo - la

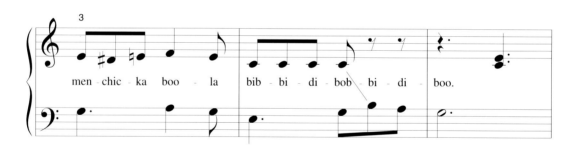

men - chic - ka - boo - la    bib - bi - di - bob - bi - di - boo.

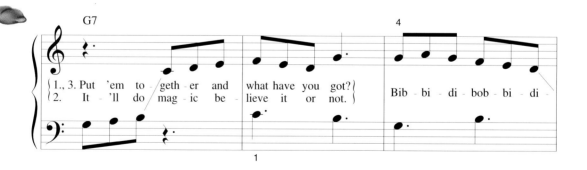

1., 3. Put 'em to - geth - er and    what have you got?
2. It 'll do    mag - ic be - lieve it or not.    Bib - bi - di - bob - bi - di -

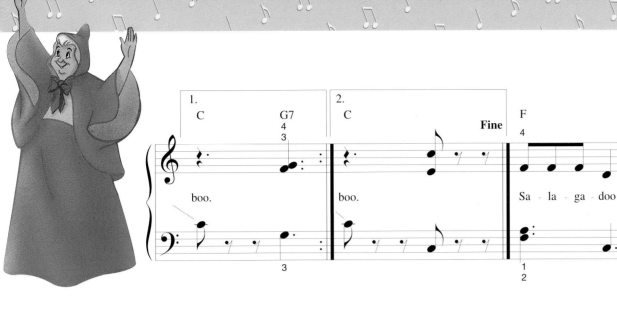

boo.

boo.

Sa - la - ga - doo - la

means

men - chic - ka - boo - le - roo, but the

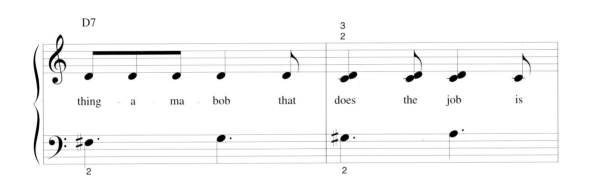

thing - a - ma - bob that does the job is

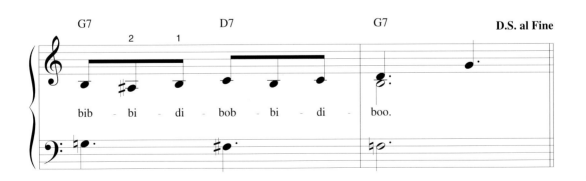

**D.S. al Fine**

bib - bi - di - bob - bi - di - boo.

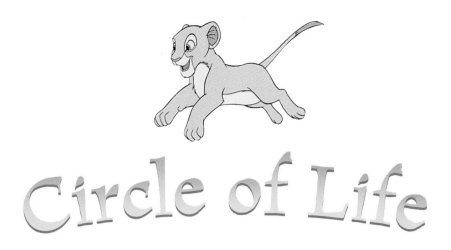

# Circle of Life

## From Walt Disney Pictures' *The Lion King*

### Music by Elton John • Lyrics by Tim Rice

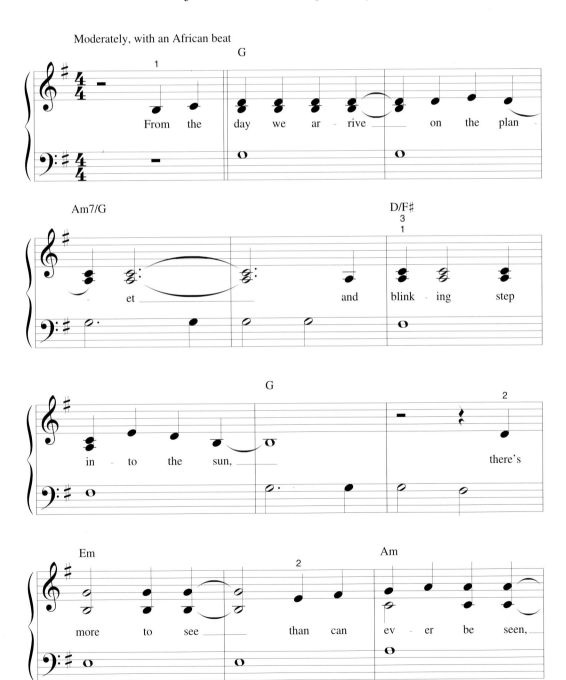

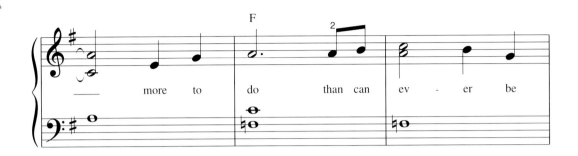

more to do than can ev - er be

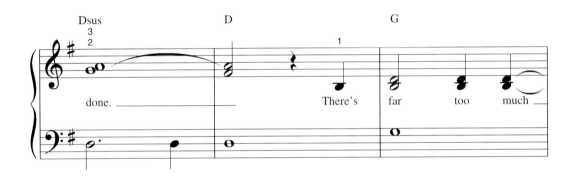

done. There's far too much

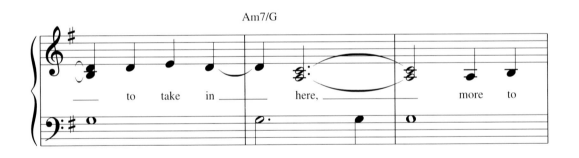

to take in here, more to

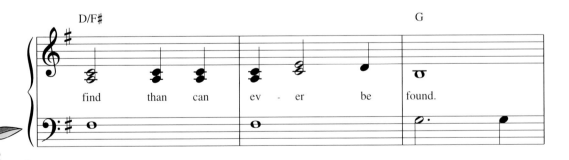

find than can ev - er be found.

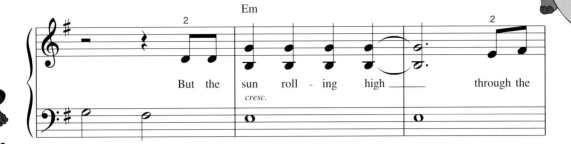

But the sun roll - ing high through the

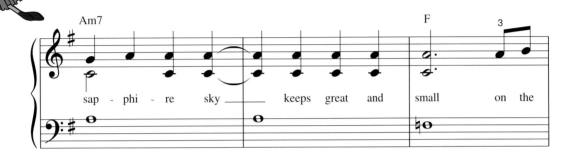

sap - phi - re sky _____ keeps great and small on the

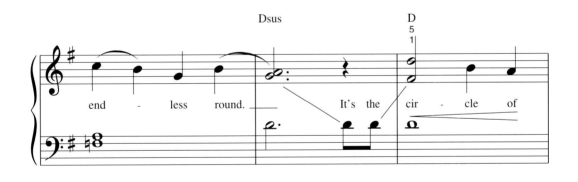

end - less round. _____ It's the cir - cle of

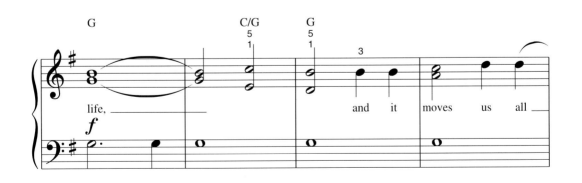

life, _____ and it moves us all

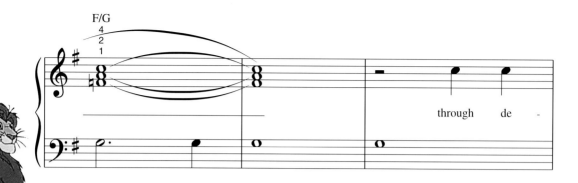

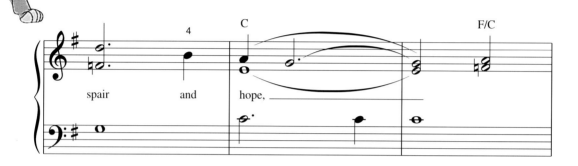

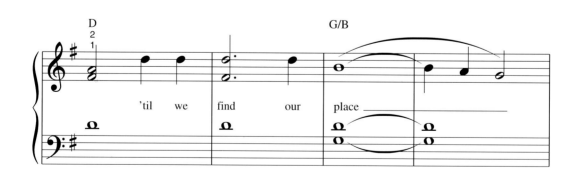

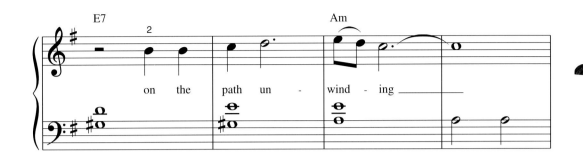

on the path un - wind - ing

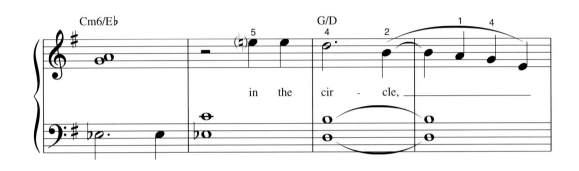

in the cir - cle,

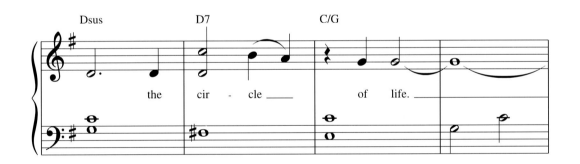

the cir - cle ___ of life. ___

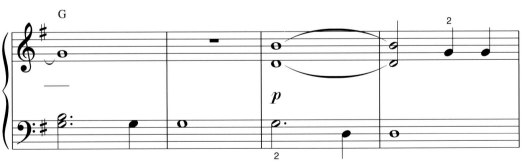

63

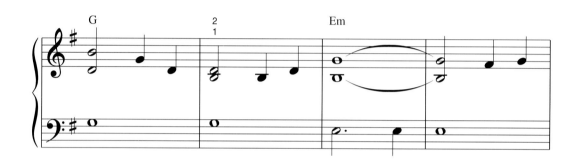

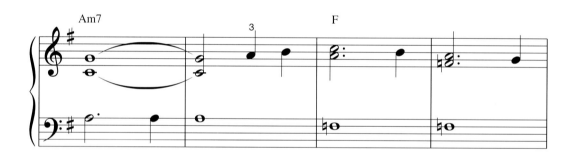

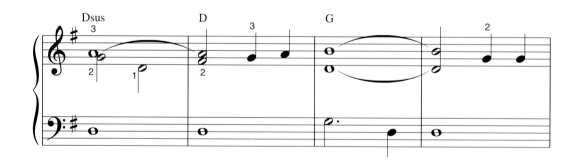

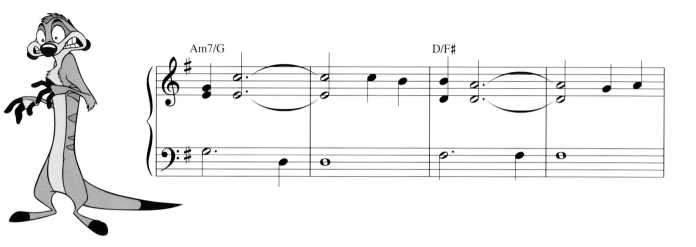

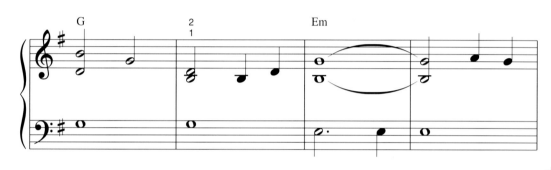

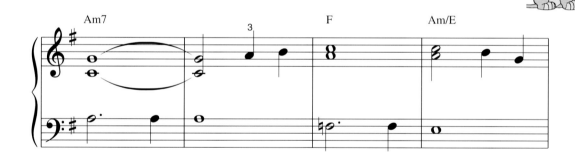

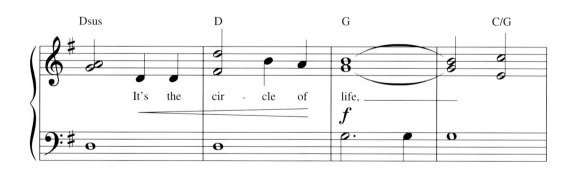

It's the cir - cle of life, _____

*f*

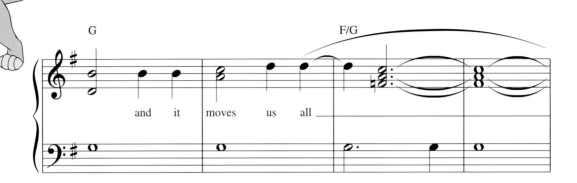

and it moves us all

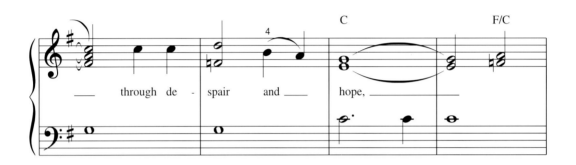

through de - spair and hope,

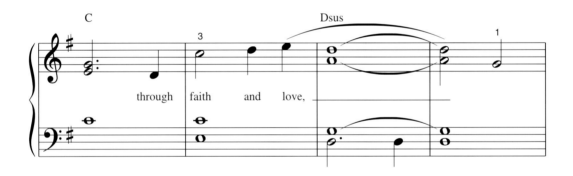

through faith and love,

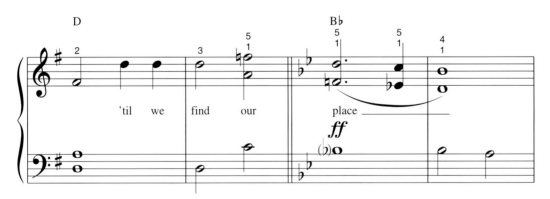

'til we find our place

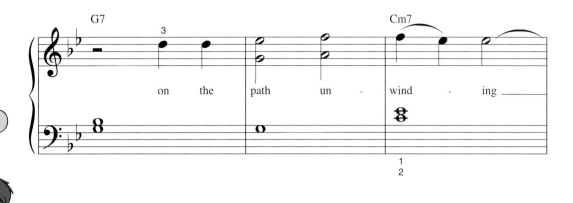

on the    path    un -    wind -    ing

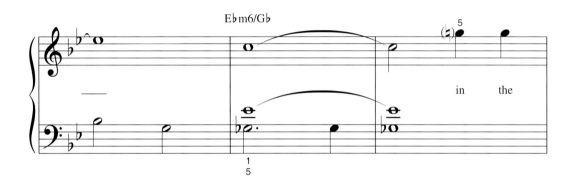

in    the

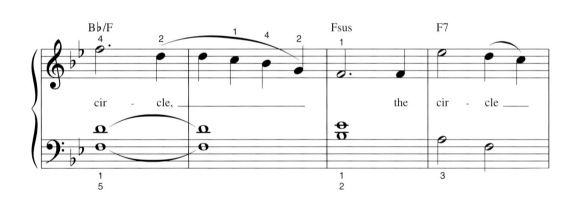

cir - cle,    the    cir - cle

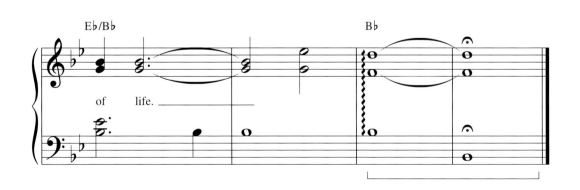

of    life.

# Hakuna Matata

## From Walt Disney Pictures' *The Lion King*

### Music by Elton John • Lyrics by Tim Rice

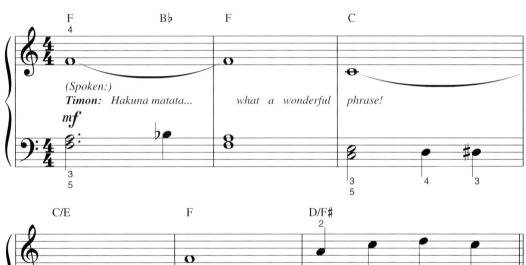

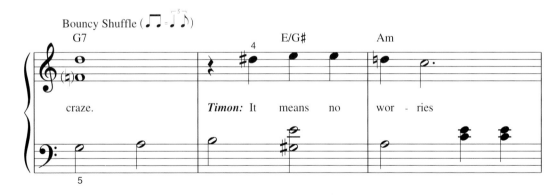

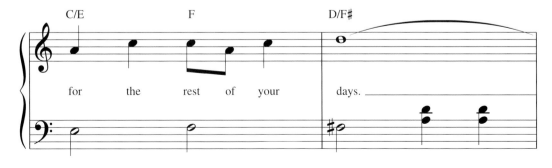

69

**Timon &
Pumbaa:** It's our prob-lem - free _____ phi -

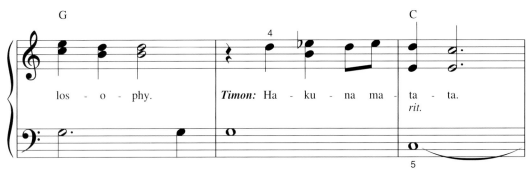

los - o - phy. **Timon:** Ha - ku - na ma - ta - ta.
*rit.*

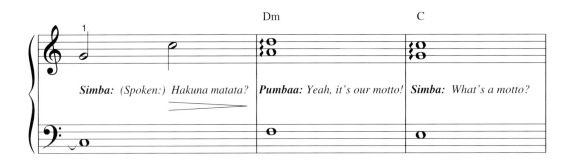

**Simba:** *(Spoken:) Hakuna matata?* | **Pumbaa:** *Yeah, it's our motto!* | **Simba:** *What's a motto?*

**Timon:** *Nothin'! What's a motta with you? (Laughter)* | **Pumbaa:** *Y'know kid, these*

two words will solve all your problems. **Timon:** *That's right. Take Pumbaa for example.  Why,*  when

*f*

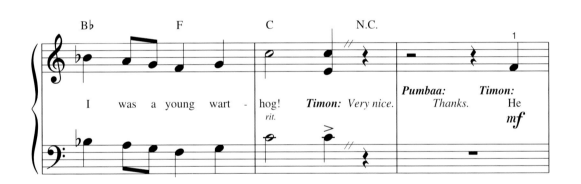

he    was    a    young    wart - hog...    ***Pumbaa:*** *When*

*ff*

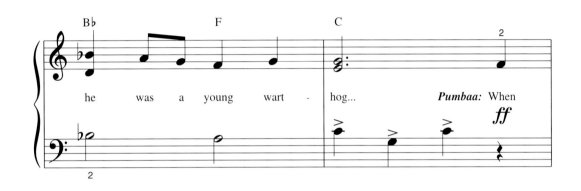

I    was    a    young    wart - hog!    ***Timon:*** *Very nice.*    ***Pumbaa:*** *Thanks.*    ***Timon:*** He

*rit.*

*mf*

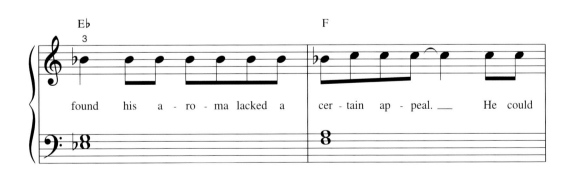

found    his    a - ro - ma    lacked    a    cer - tain    ap - peal. ___    He could

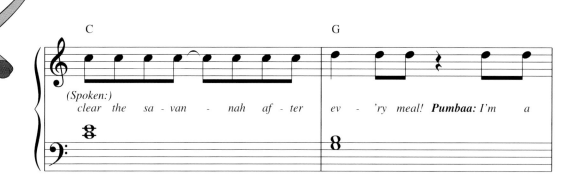

*(Spoken:)*
clear the sa - van - - nah af - ter | ev - 'ry meal! **Pumbaa:** I'm a

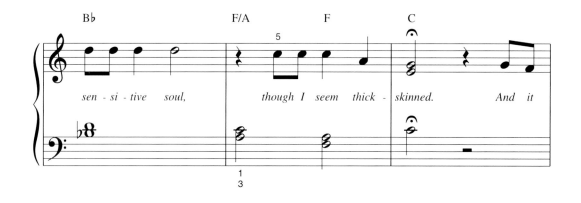

sen - si - tive soul, | though I seem thick - skinned. | And it

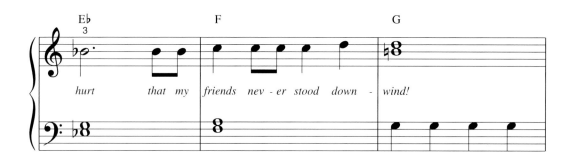

hurt | that my | friends nev - er stood down - wind!

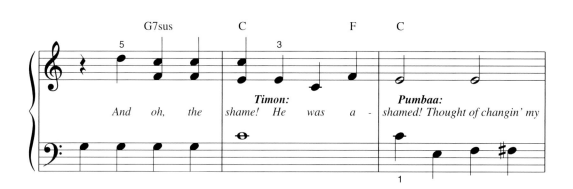

And oh, the | shame! He was a - | *shamed!* Thought of changin' my

**Timon:** | **Pumbaa:**

**Timon:**
name! Oh, what's in a name? And I got down-heart-ed... How did you

**Pumbaa:**

**Timon:**

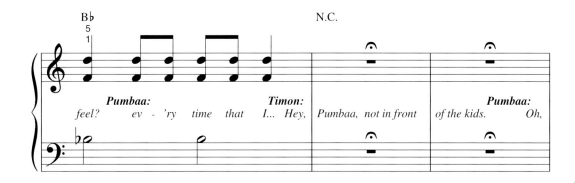

**Pumbaa:**
feel? ev-'ry time that I... Hey, Pumbaa, not in front of the kids. Oh,

**Timon:**

**Pumbaa:**

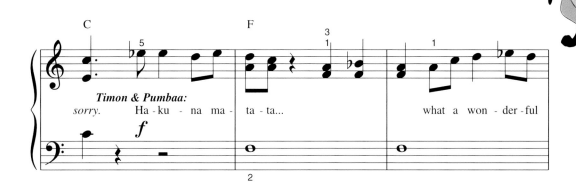

**Timon & Pumbaa:**
sorry. Ha-ku-na ma-ta-ta... what a won-der-ful

phrase. Ha-ku-na ma-ta-ta...

ain't no pass - ing craze. *Simba:* It means no

wor - ries for the rest of your days. _____
*Timon:* Yeah, sing it kid!

*Timon &*
*Simba:* It's our prob -lem - free _____ *Pumbaa:* phi -

los - o - phy. *Timon & Pumbaa:* Ha - ku - na ma - ta - ta.

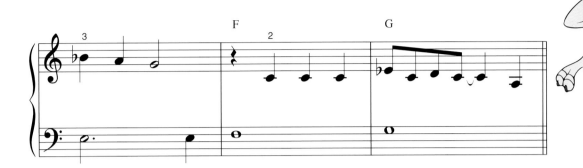

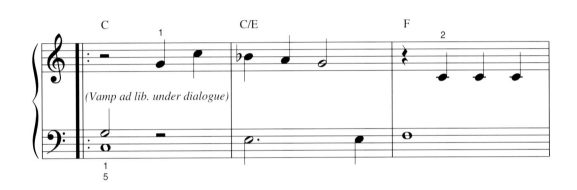

(Vamp ad lib. under dialogue)

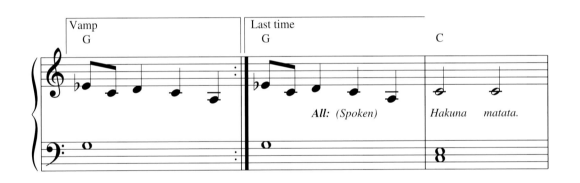

Vamp

Last time

*All:* (Spoken)  Hakuna     matata.

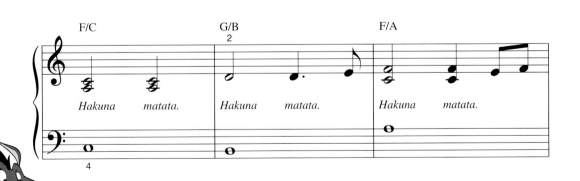

Hakuna     matata.     Hakuna     matata.     Hakuna     matata.

C/G                      G

*Hakuna matata. Hakuna matata. Hakuna matata.*

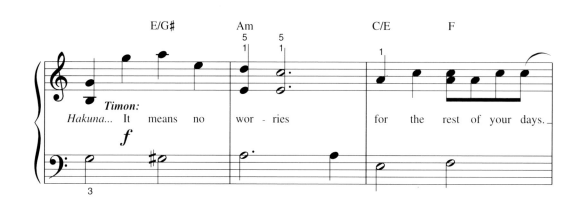

E/G♯       Am             C/E      F

***Timon:***
*Hakuna... It means no wor - ries*     *for the rest of your days.*

*f*

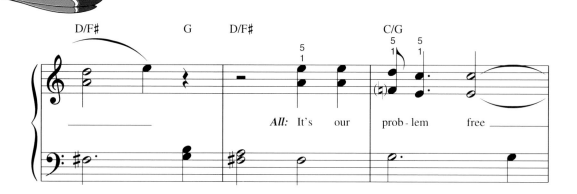

D/F♯       G     D/F♯        C/G

***All:*** *It's our prob - lem free*

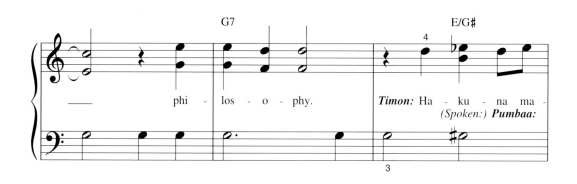

G7                    E/G♯

*phi - los - o - phy.*     ***Timon:*** *Ha - ku - na ma -*
                                    *(Spoken:)* ***Pumbaa:***

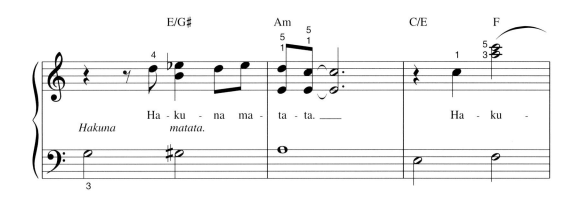

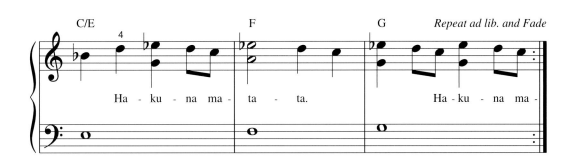

# Beauty and the Beast

From Walt Disney's *Beauty and the Beast*

Lyrics by Howard Ashman • Music by Alan Menken

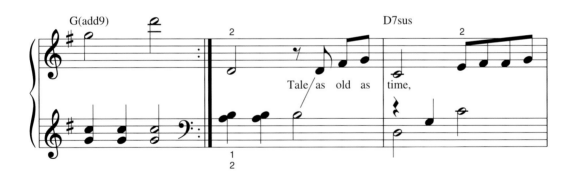

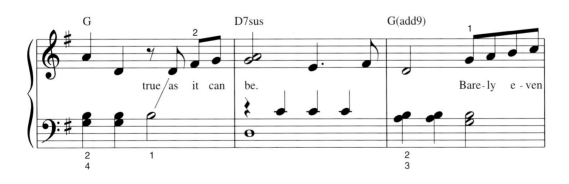

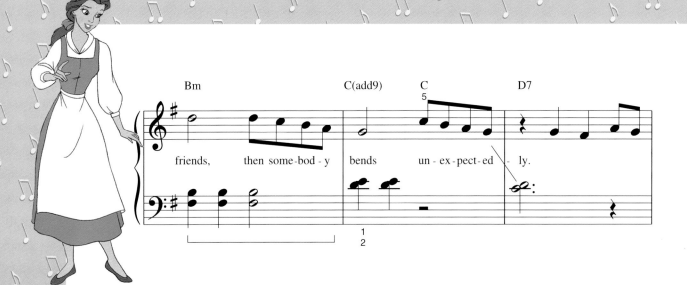

friends, then some-bod-y bends un-ex-pect-ed - ly.

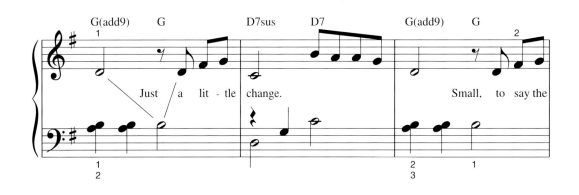

Just a lit - tle change. Small, to say the

least. Both a lit - tle scared, nei-ther one pre - pared. Beau-ty and the

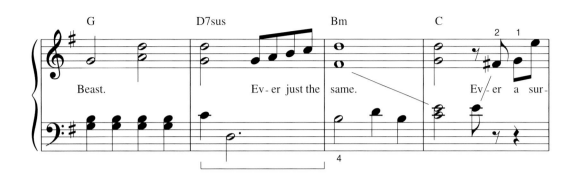

Beast.      Ev - er just the   same.      Ev - er a sur-

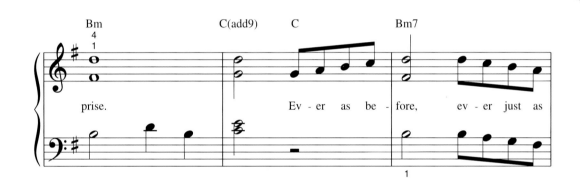

prise.      Ev - er as be - fore,   ev - er just as

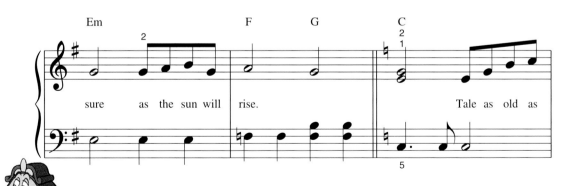

sure    as the sun will   rise.      Tale as old as

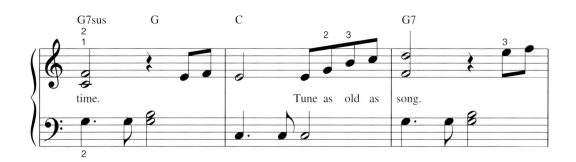

time.
Tune as old as song.

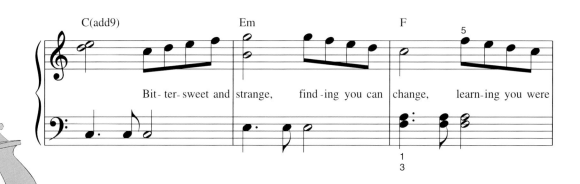

Bit-ter-sweet and strange, find-ing you can change, learn-ing you were

wrong.
Cer-tain as the sun rising

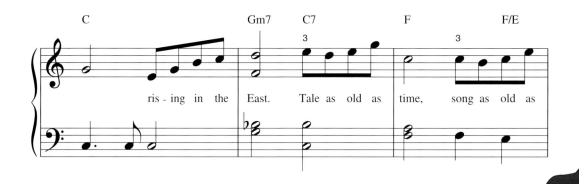

ris - ing in the East. Tale as old as time, song as old as

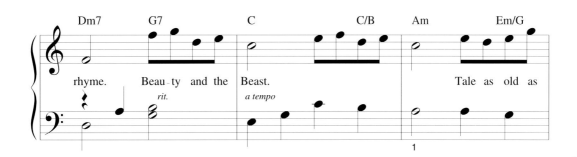

rhyme.   Beau - ty  and  the  Beast.            Tale  as  old  as

time,    song  as  old  as   rhyme.   Beau - ty  and  the  Beast.

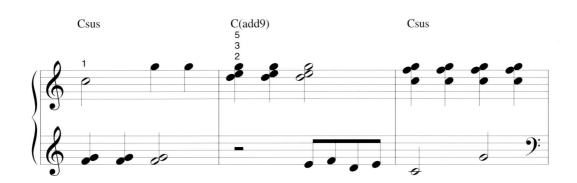

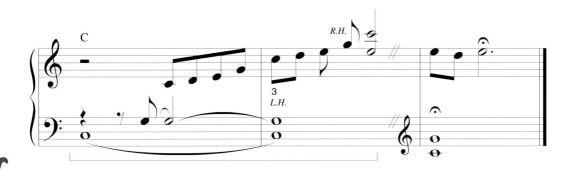

# Winnie the Pooh

**From Walt Disney's _The Many Adventures of Winnie the Pooh_**

Words and Music by Richard M. Sherman and Robert B. Sherman

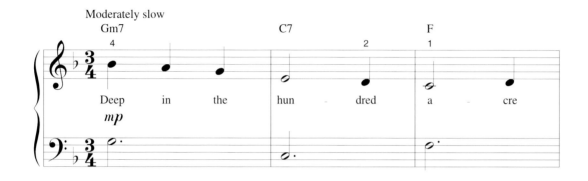

Deep in the hun - dred a - cre

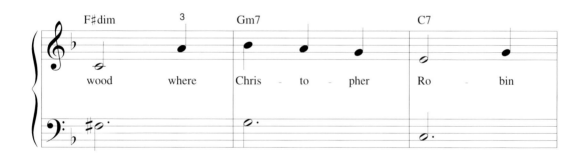

wood where Chris - to - pher Ro - bin

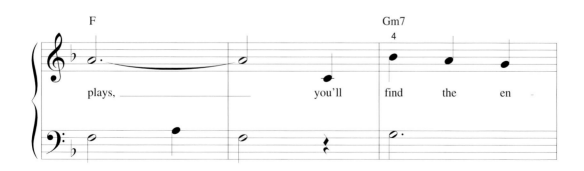

plays, _____ you'll find the en -

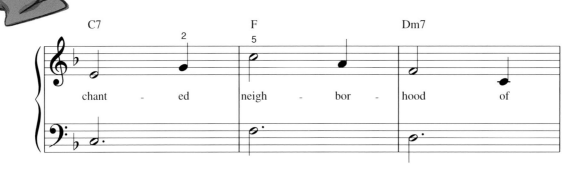

chant - ed neigh - bor - hood of

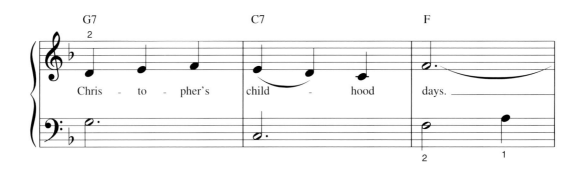

Chris - to - pher's child - hood days. ___

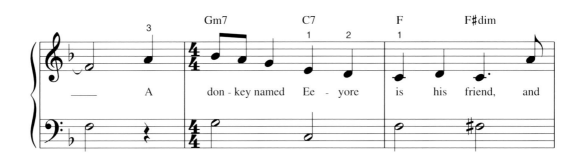

___ A don - key named Ee - yore is his friend, and

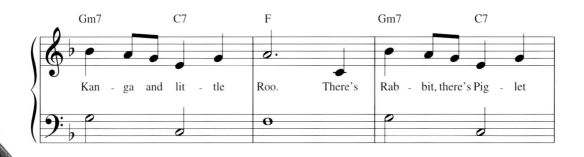

Kan - ga and lit - tle Roo. There's Rab - bit, there's Pig - let

and there's Owl, but most of all Win - nie the Pooh!

Win - nie the Pooh, Win - nie the Pooh, tub - by lit - tle cub - by all

stuffed with fluff, he's Win - nie the Pooh, Win - nie the Pooh,

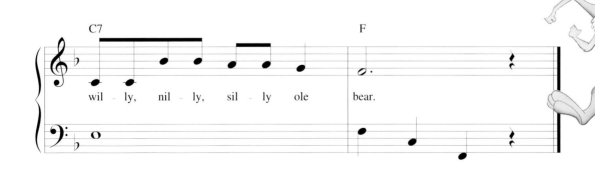

wil - ly, nil - ly, sil - ly ole bear.

# The Wonderful Thing About Tiggers

From Walt Disney's *The Many Adventures of Winnie the Pooh*

Words and Music by Richard M. Sherman and Robert B. Sherman

With a bounce (♩.=1 beat)

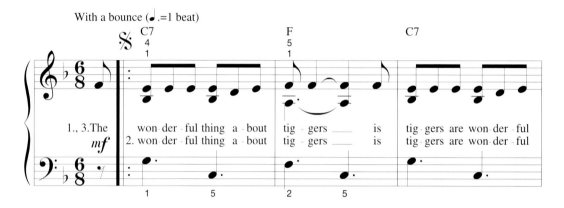

1., 3.The wonderful thing about tiggers _____ is tiggers are wonderful
2. wonderful thing about tiggers _____ is tiggers are wonderful

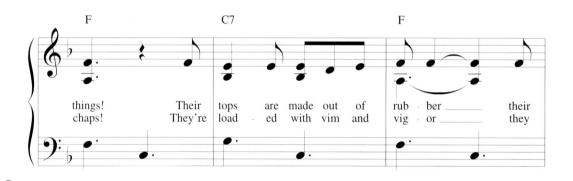

things!    Their tops    are made out of    rubber _____    their
chaps!    They're    loaded    with vim and    vigor _____    they

bottoms are made out of    springs. _____    They're bouncy, trouncy,
love    to leap in your    laps. _____    They're jumpy, bumpy,

foun - cy, poun - cy,
clump - y, thump - y,
fun! Fun! Fun! Fun! Fun! But the most won-der-ful

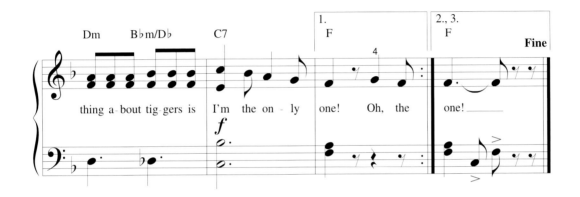

thing a-bout tig-gers is I'm the on - ly one! Oh, the one!

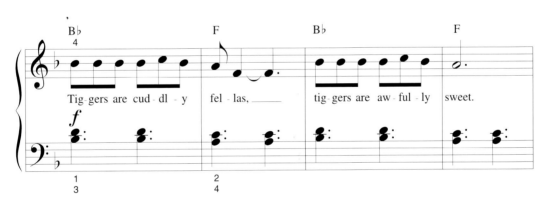

Tig-gers are cud-dl - y fel - las, tig-gers are aw-ful-ly sweet.

Ev-'ry-one else is jea-lous. That's why I re - peat and re-peat: The

# GO THE DISTANCE

From Walt Disney Pictures' *Hercules*

Music by Alan Menken • Lyrics by David Zippel

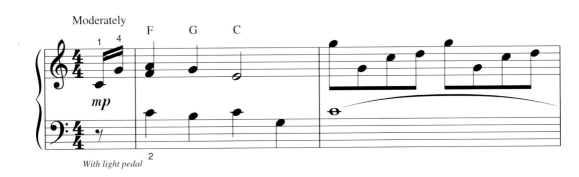

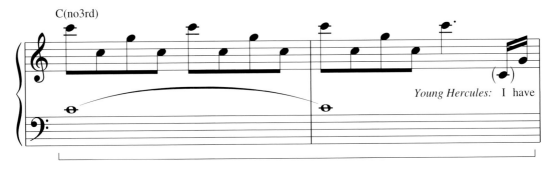

*Young Hercules:* I have

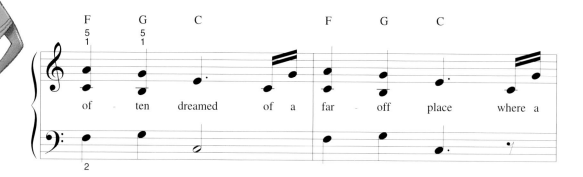

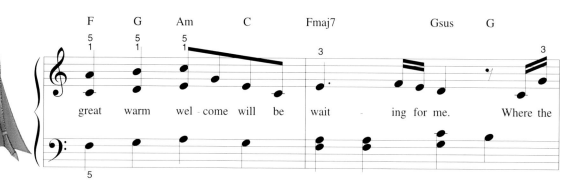

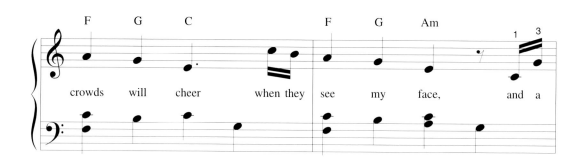

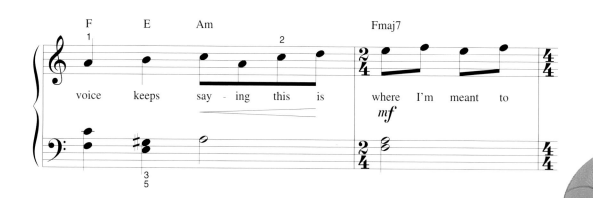

be. _____ I will find my way.

I can go the dis - tance. I'll be there some - day

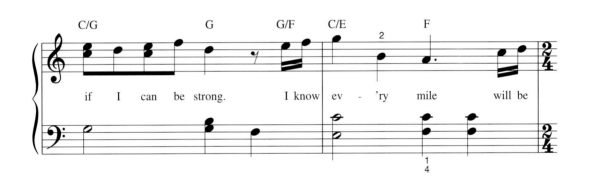

if I can be strong. I know ev - 'ry mile will be

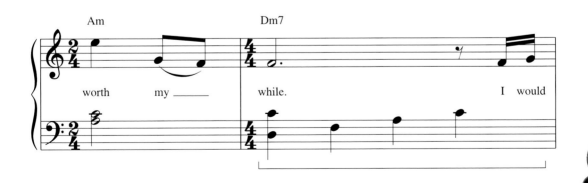

worth my _____ while. I would

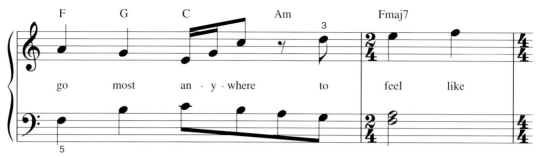

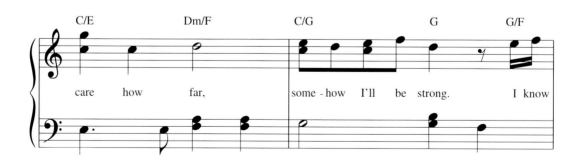

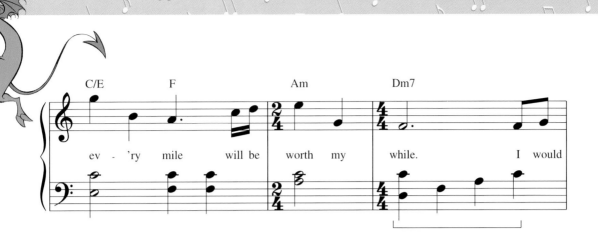

ev - 'ry mile will be worth my while. I would

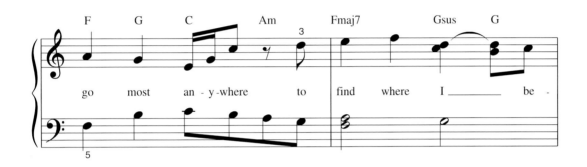

go most an - y-where to find where I _____ be -

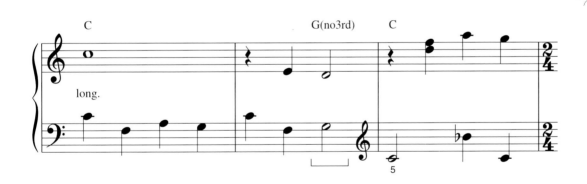

long.

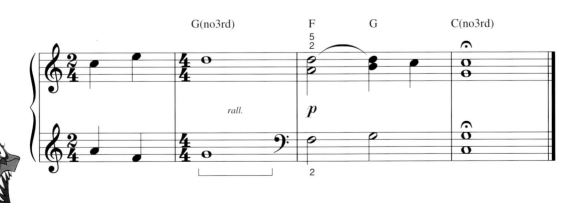

Used by permission. All rights reserved. Credit and copyright notices for each song appear on the first page of that song.
Co-published in 1998 by Hal Leonard Publishing Corporation, Milwaukee, Wisconsin and Disney Press, New York.

Printed in Singapore.
First Edition
1 3 5 7 9 10 8 6 4 2
Library of Congress Catalog Card Number 97-66885
ISBN: 0-7868-3147-2 (trade) —0-7868-5071-x (lib. bdg.)